PIANO SOLO

Latin Standards

ISBN 0-634-06939-X

HAL•LEONARD®
CORPORATION

7777 W. BLUEMOUND RD. P.O. BOX 13819 MILWAUKEE, WI 53213

Visit Hal Leonard Online at
www.halleonard.com

Latin Standards

4   A FELICIDADE

11   AGUA DE BEBER (WATER TO DRINK)

16   AMOR (AMOR, AMOR, AMOR)

21   AQUELLOS OJOS VERDES (GREEN EYES)

26   BAIA (BAHÍA)

36   BÉSAME MUCHO (KISS ME MUCH)

40   THE GIFT! (RECADO BOSSA NOVA)

31   THE GIRL FROM IPANEMA (GARÔTA DE IPANEMA)

46   HOW INSENSITIVE (INSENSATEZ)

50   MEDITATION (MEDITACÃO)

54   SO NICE (SUMMER SAMBA)

62   SWAY (QUIEN SERÁ)

57   TICO TICO (TICO TICO NO FUBA)

68   WATCH WHAT HAPPENS

73   WAVE

A FELICIDADE

Words and Music by VINICIUS DE MORAES,
ANDRE SALVET and ANTONIO CARLOS JOBIM

Bright Bossa Nova

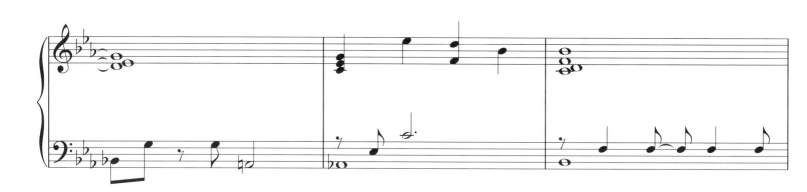

Slower

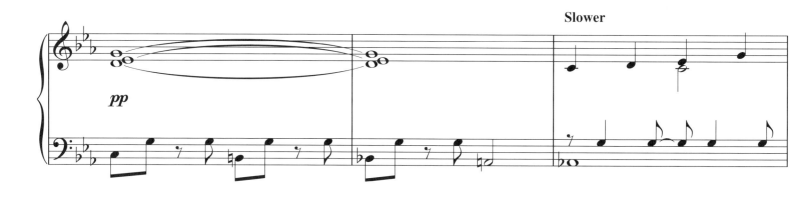

AGUA DE BEBER
(Water to Drink)

English Words by NORMAN GIMBEL
Portuguese Words by VINICIUS DE MORAES
Music by ANTONIO CARLOS JOBIM

Soulfully

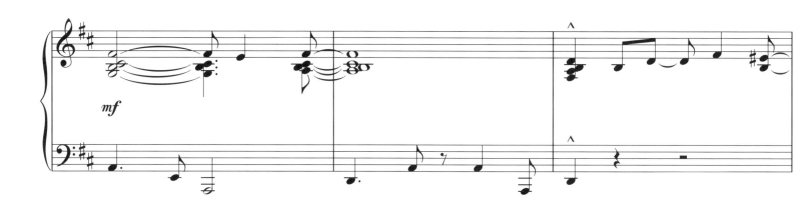

AMOR
(Amor, Amor, Amor)

Music by GABRIEL RUIZ
Spanish Words by RICARDO LOPEZ MENDEZ
English Words by NORMAN NEWELL

Beguine

Tempo I

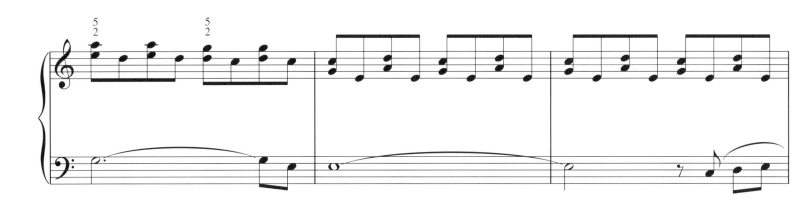

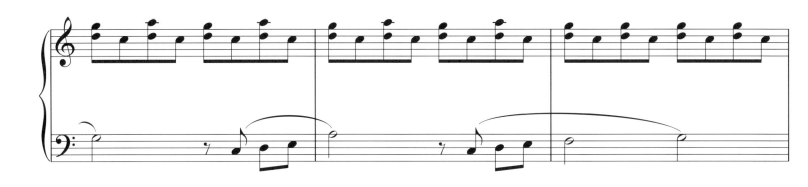

AQUELLOS OJOS VERDES
(Green Eyes)

Music by NILO MENENDEZ
Spanish Words by ADOLFO UTRERA
English Words by E. RIVERA and E. WOODS

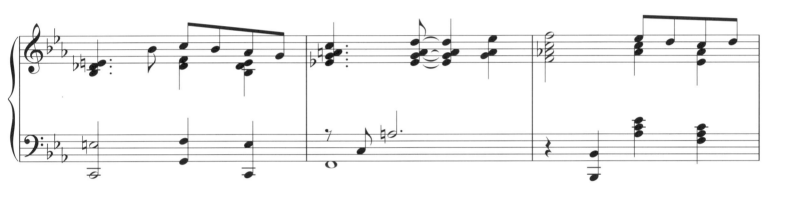

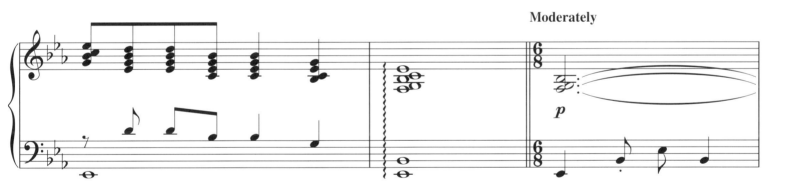

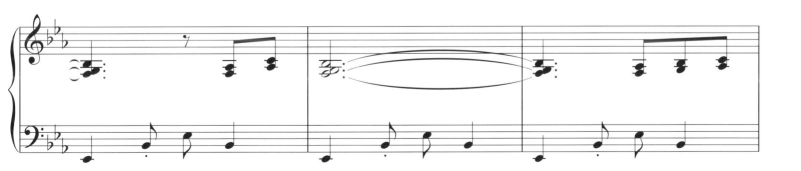

A Tempo Bossa Nova

BAIA
(Bahía)

Music and Portuguese Lyric by ARY BARROSO
English Lyric by RAY GILBERT

THE GIRL FROM IPANEMA
(Garôta De Ipanema)

Music by ANTONIO CARLOS JOBIM
English Words by NORMAN GIMBEL
Original Words by VINICIUS DE MORAES

Moderately

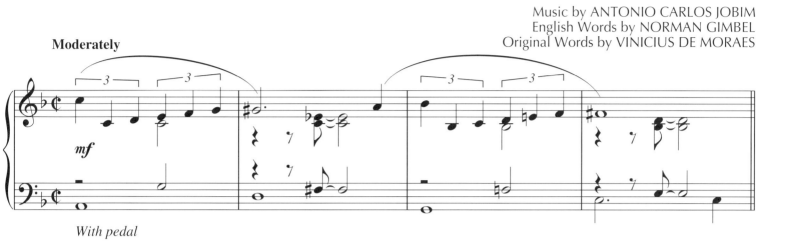

With pedal

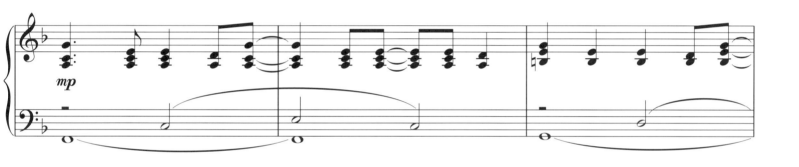

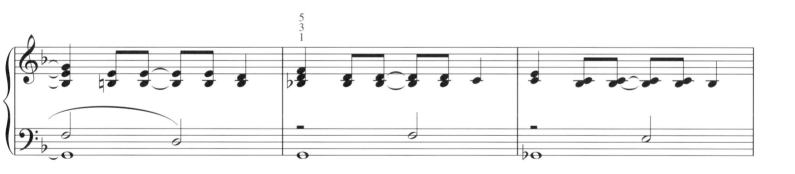

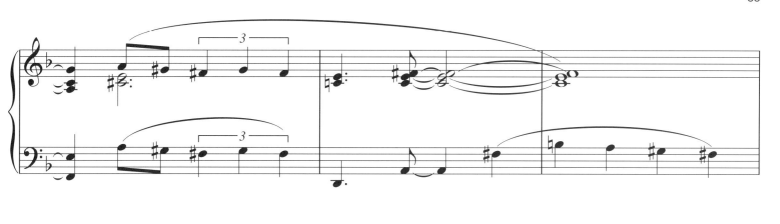

no pedal

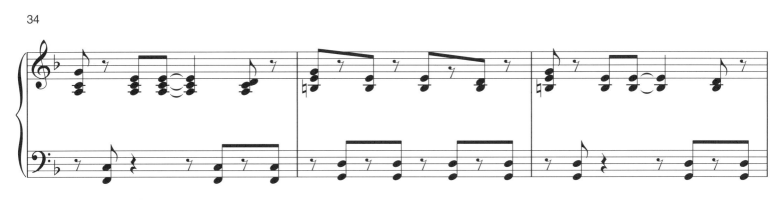

add pedal

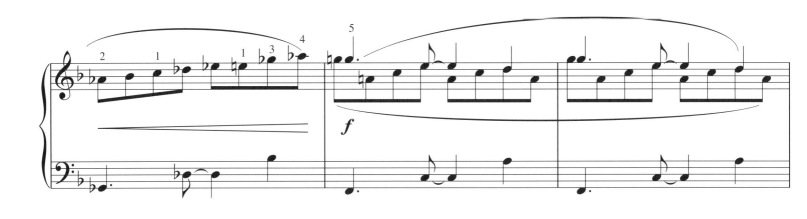

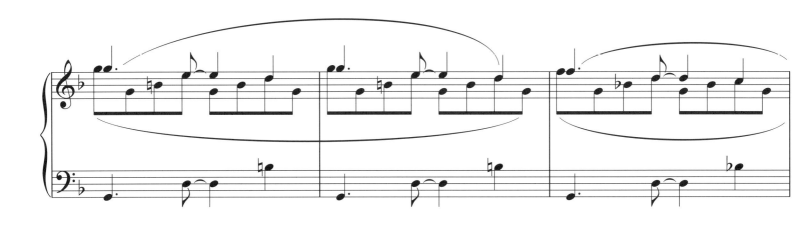

BÉSAME MUCHO
(Kiss Me Much)

Music and Spanish Words by CONSUELO VELAZQUEZ
English Words by SUNNY SKYLAR

Freely

Moderately, not too fast

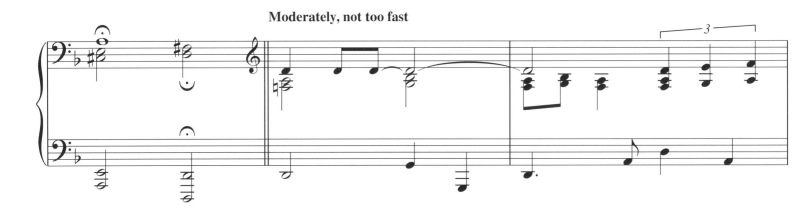

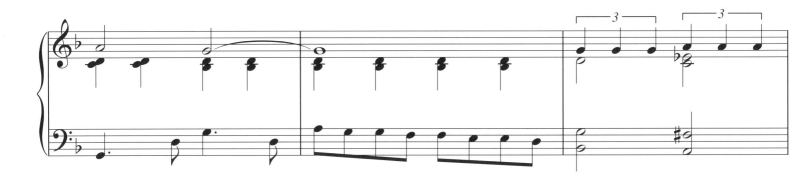

THE GIFT!
(Recado Bossa Nova)

Music by DJALMA FERREIRA
Original Lyric by LUIZ ANTONIO
English Lyric by PAUL FRANCIS WEBSTER

Bright Bossa

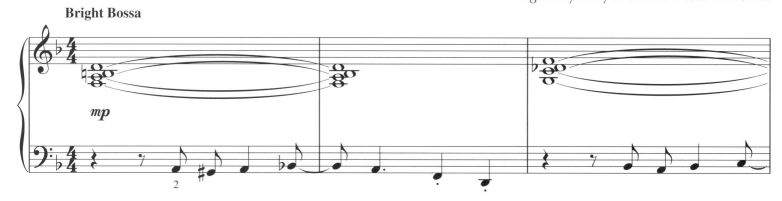

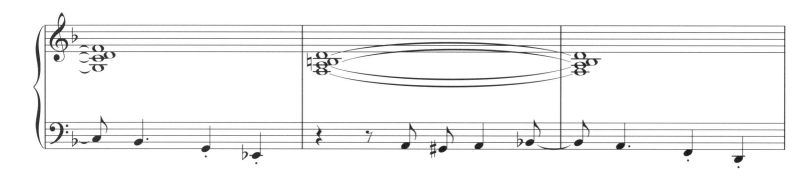

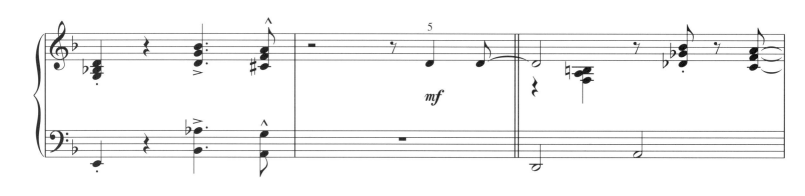

HOW INSENSITIVE
(Insensatez)

Music by ANTONIO CARLOS JOBIM
Original Words by VINICIUS DE MORAES
English Words by NORMAN GIMBEL

Moderately slow

mp

With pedal

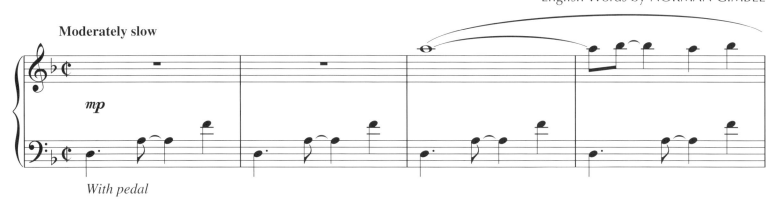

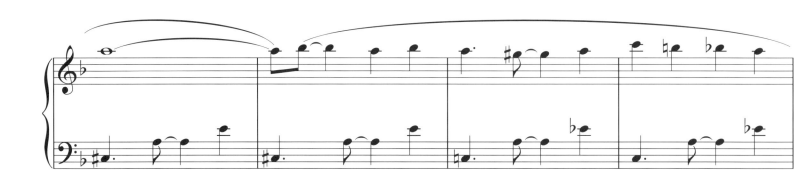

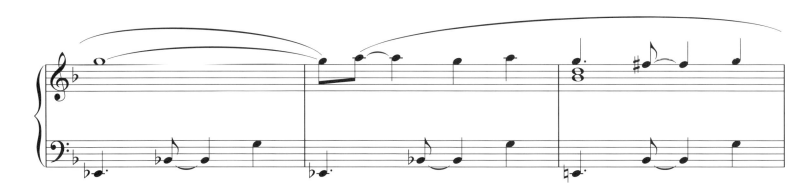

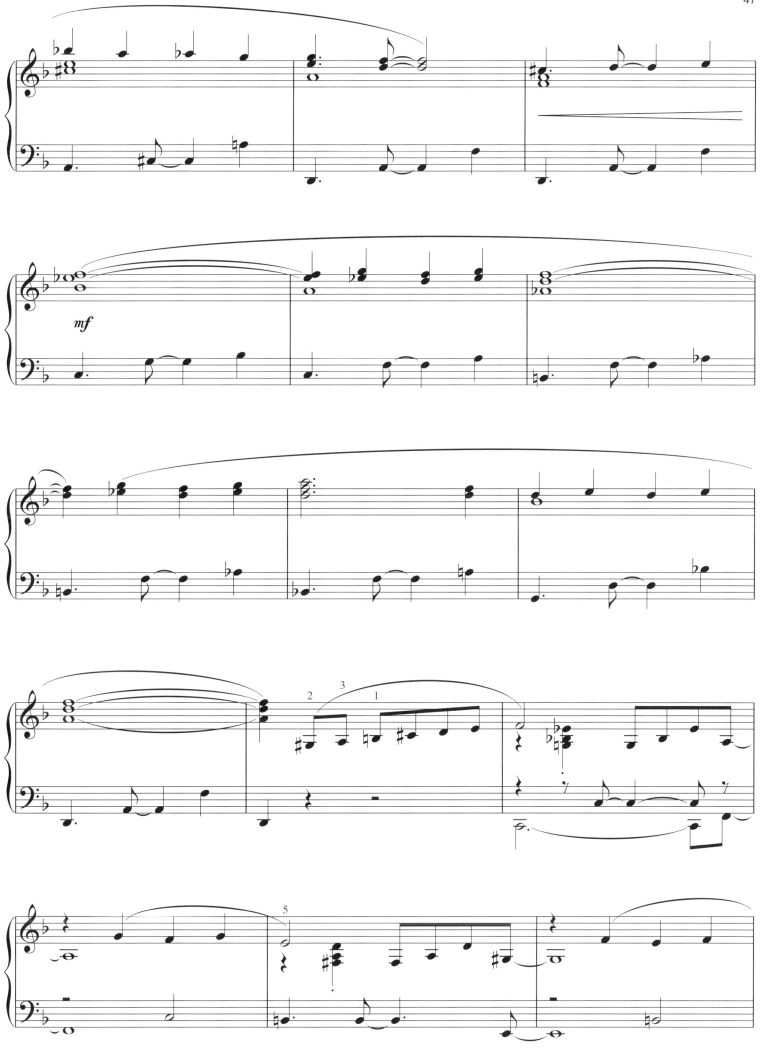

MEDITATION
(Meditacão)

Music by ANTONIO CARLOS JOBIM
Original Words by NEWTON MENDONCA
English Words by NORMAN GIMBEL

Relaxed Bossa Nova

To Coda ⊕

D.S. al Coda

mp *f*

CODA

SO NICE
(Summer Samba)

Original Words and Music by MARCOS VALLE
and PAULO SERGIO VALLE
English Words by NORMAN GIMBEL

Medium Bossa Nova

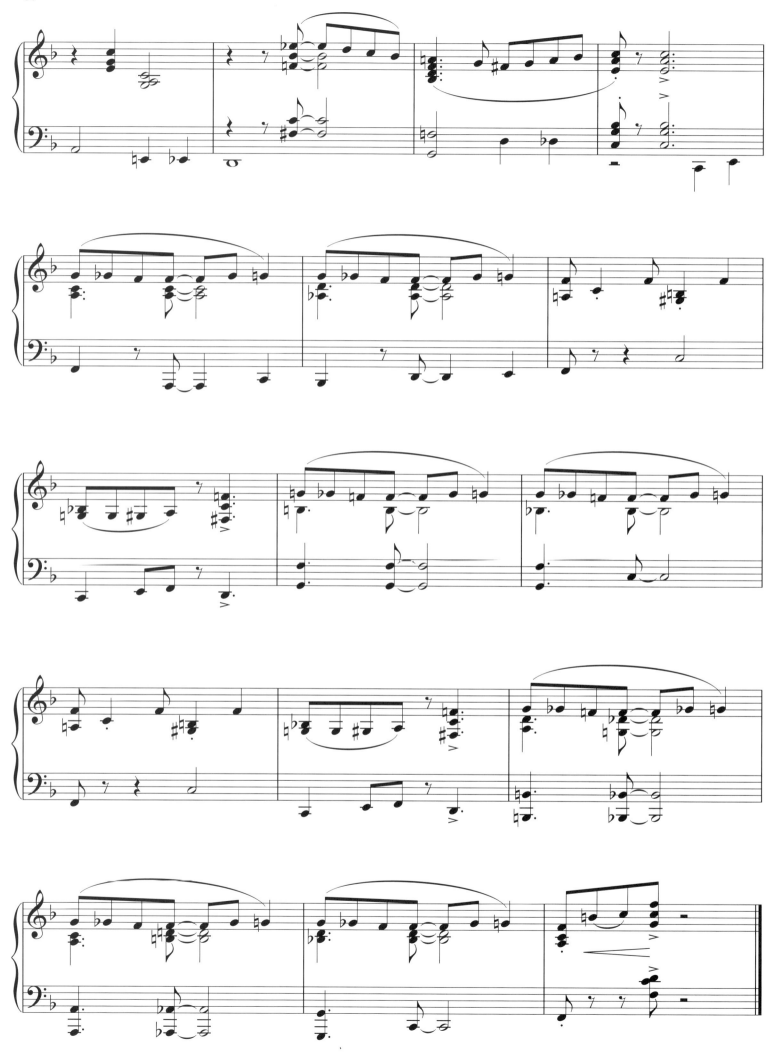

TICO TICO
(Tico Tico No Fuba)

Words and Music by ZEQUINHA ABREU,
ALOYSIO OLIVEIRA and ERVIN DRAKE

Brightly

58

Tempo I

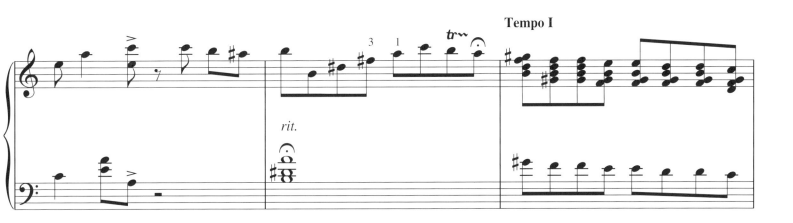

D.S. al Coda

CODA **Slower**

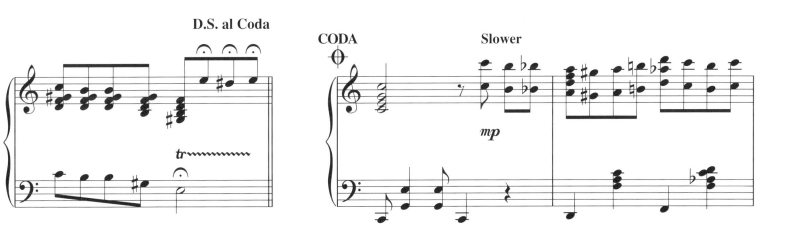

Tempo I

8va

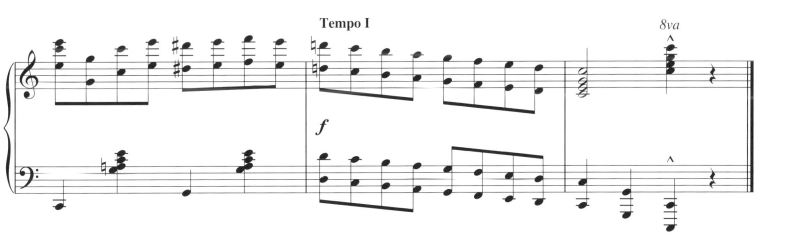

SWAY
(Quien Será)

English Words by NORMAN GIMBEL
Spanish Words and Music by PABLO BELTRAN RUIZ

Moderate Tango

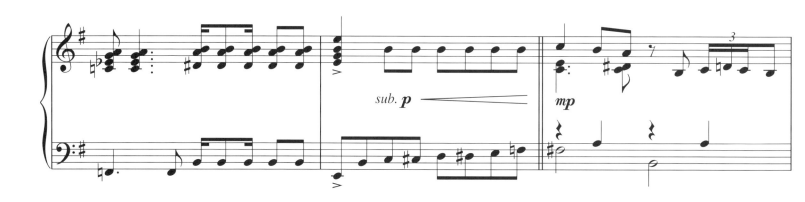

WATCH WHAT HAPPENS
from THE UMBRELLAS OF CHERBOURG

Music by MICHEL LEGRAND
Original French Text by JACQUES DEMY
English Lyrics by NORMAN GIMBEL

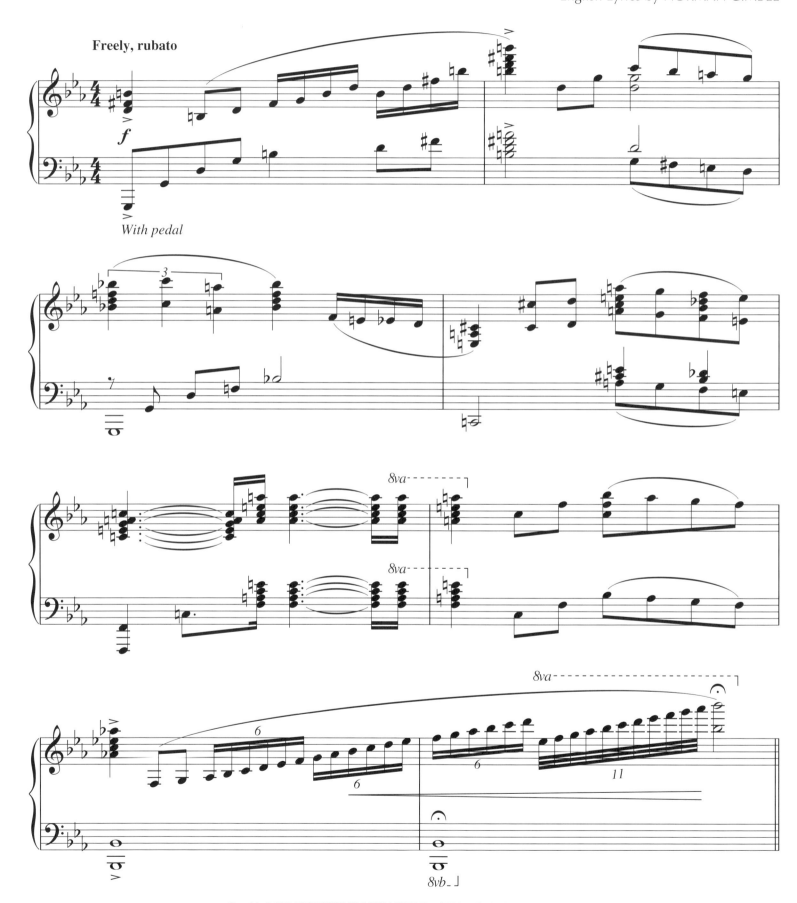

Easy Bossa Nova

71

WAVE

Words and Music by
ANTONIO CARLOS JOBIM

mp

With pedal

YOUR FAVORITE MUSIC

ARRANGED FOR PIANO SOLO

Broadway – 20 Piano Solos
Play rich piano solo arrangements of 20 Broadway favorites! Includes: All I Ask of You • And All That Jazz • Can You Feel the Love Tonight • Edelweiss • The Impossible Deam • Memory • On My Own • Put On a Happy Face • Seasons of Love • Some Enchanted Evening • Summer Nights • Tomorrow • Unexpected Song • and more!
00311028 ....$12.95

Classic Broadway Solos
16 beautifully arranged Broadway standards including: I Could Have Danced All Night • If Ever I Would Leave You • The Impossible Dream • Memory • Smoke Gets in Your Eyes • You'll Never Walk Alone • and more.

00294002 ....$12.95

Classical Themes from the Movies
Over 31 familiar and favorite themes, including: Also Sprach Zarathustra • Ave Maria • Canon in D • Habanera • Overture to *The Marriage of Figaro* • and more.

00221010 ....$9.95

Definitive Classical Collection
129 selections. Includes music by Johann Sebastian Bach, Ludwig van Beethoven, Johannes Brahms, Frederic Chopin, Claude Debussy, George Frideric Handel, Felix Mendelssohn, Johann Pachelbel, Franz Schubert, Pyotr Tchaikovsky, Richard Wagner, and many more!
00310772 ....$29.95

Jazz Standards
15 all-time favorite songs, including: All The Things You Are • Bluesette • I'll Remember April • Mood Indigo • Satin Doll • and more.

00292055 ....$12.95

Billy Joel Easy Classics
This unique collection includes 17 of his best songs: Honesty • It's Still Rock and Roll to Me • The Longest Time • Movin' Out (Anthony's Song) • My Life • Piano Man • Roberta • She's Got a Way • Uptown Girl • more.
00306202 ....$12.95

Lennon & McCartney Piano Solos
22 beautiful arrangements, including: Eleanor Rigby • The Fool on the Hill • Here, There and Everywhere • Lady Madonna • Let It Be • Yesterday • and more.
00294023 ....$14.95

Andrew Lloyd Webber
14 pieces, including: All I Ask of You • Don't Cry for Me Argentina • Memory • The Music of the Night • Phantom of the Opera • Pie Jesu • and more.

00292001 ....$14.95

Love & Wedding Piano Solos
26 contemporary and classic wedding favorites, including: All I Ask of You • Ave Maria • Endless Love • Through the Years • Vision of Love • Sunrise, Sunset • Don't Know Much • Unchained Melody • and more.

00311507 ....$12.95

Memorable Jazz Standards
24 elegant favorites: Autumn in New York • Autumn Leaves • Body and Soul • How Deep Is the Ocean • Isn't It Romantic? • It Might as Well Be Spring • My Funny Valentine • Satin Doll • Stella by Starlight • The Very Thought of You • When I Fall in Love • more.
00310719 ....$12.95

Movie Piano Solos
20 rich arrangements, including: The Exodus Song • The Firm Main Title • The Godfather (Love Theme) • Moon River • Raider's March • Theme From Schindler's List • When I Fall in Love • A Whole New World • and more.

00311675 ....$10.95

Elvis Presley Pianos Solos
A great collection of over 15 of The King's best, including: Are You Lonesome Tonight? • Don't Be Cruel • It's Now or Never • Love Me Tender • All Shook Up • and more.

00292002 ....$9.95

Sacred Inspirations
arr. Phillip Keveren
11 songs, featuring: How Majestic Is Your Name • Great Is the Lord • Amazing Grace • Friends • Via Dolorosa • In the Name of the Lord • and more.

00292057 ....$9.95

Shout to the Lord
Moving arrangements of 14 praise favorites as interpreted by Phillip Keveren: As the Deer • El Shaddai • How Beautiful • How Majestic Is Your Name • More Precious Than Silver • Oh Lord, You're Beautiful • Shine, Jesus, Shine • Shout to the Lord • and more.
00310699 ....$12.95

Showcase for Piano
Intermediate to advanced arrangements of 18 popular songs: Bali Ha'i • Bewitched • I Can't Get Started with You • I Could Write a Book • I'll Be Seeing You • My Funny Valentine • September Song • Where or When • You'll Never Walk Alone • and more.

00310664 ....$8.95

TV Themes
33 classic themes, including: Addams Family • Alfred Hitchcock Presents • The Brady Bunch • (Meet) The Flintstones • Home Improvement • Mister Ed • Northern Exposure • This Is It (Bugs Bunny Theme) • Twin Peaks • and more.

00292030 ....$10.95

FOR MORE INFORMATION, SEE YOUR LOCAL MUSIC DEALER, OR WRITE TO:

HAL•LEONARD® CORPORATION
7777 W. BLUEMOUND RD. P.O. BOX 13819 MILWAUKEE, WI 53213

Visit Hal Leonard online at **www.halleonard.com**

*Prices, contents, and availability subject to change without notice.
Some products may not be available outside the U.S.A.*

0504

LA SERIE ¡PURA!

This exciting series profiles the many styles of Latin music. Each folio contains 25 top hits from its specific genre for piano/vocal/guitar. $14.95 each!

PURA BACHATA

Inviting collection of 25 love songs set to bachata, a highly popular rhythm from the Dominican Republic that features gentle percussion fills and tinkly guitar lines. Includes: Aquí Conmigo • Dos Locos • Tú Eres Ajena • Yo Sí Me Enamoré • Extraño A Mi Pueblo • Se Fue Mi Amor • and more.

00310946 Piano/Vocal/Guitar $14.95

PURO MERENGUE

This foremost collection contains a bevy of 25 sizzling fan favorites, including: Suavemente • Tu Sonrisa • Bajo La Lluvia • Pégame Tu Vício • Yo Te Confieso • Cuando Acaba El Placer • Bandida • Corazon De Mujer • El Tiburón • La Ventanita • Mi Reina • Niña Bonita • and more.

00310948 Piano/Vocal/Guitar $14.95

PURA CUMBIA

First-rate compendium spotlighting Colombia's famous lilting groove. 25 songs, including: La Pollera Colerá • Mete Y Saca • A Mi Dios Todo Le Debo • Tabaco Y Ron • Cumbia De Mi Tierra • Distancia • Guepaje • La Oaxaqueña • Luz De Cumbia • Maruja • Soledad • and more.

00310947 Piano/Vocal/Guitar....................$14.95

PURO TEJANO

Tejano evergreens by Los Kumbia Kings and Selena headline this exclusive set. 25 songs, including: SSHHH!! • Amor Prohibido • Azúcar • Como Flor • Boom Boom • Fotos Y Recuerdos • Baila Esta Cumbia • Costumbres • Me Estoy Enamorando • Te Quiero A Tí • and more.

00310950 Piano/Vocal/Guitar...................$14.95

PURA SALSA

A peerless collection of 25 salsa chestnuts, including: A Puro Dolor • Pena De Amor • Celos • Déjate Querer • No Morirá • Qué Hay De Malo • Si La Ves • Una Aventura • Cuando Faltas Tú • Micaela • Por Ese Hombre • Tu Recuerdo • and more.

00310949 Piano/Vocal/Guitar....................$14.95

PURO VALLENATO

Kinetic, accordion-powered classics from Colombia's Atlantic coast. 25 songs, including: Déjame Entrar • El Santo Cachón • Fruta Fresca • Alicia Adorada • No Pude Quitarte Las Espinas • Aquí Conmigo • Embrujo • Festival En Guararé • La Patillalera • Luna Nueva • Pedazo De Acordeón • Tierra Mala • and more.

00310951 Piano/Vocal/Guitar....................$14.95

Prices, contents, and availability subject to change without notice.

FOR MORE INFORMATION, SEE YOUR LOCAL MUSIC DEALER, OR WRITE TO:

HAL•LEONARD®
CORPORATION
7777 W. BLUEMOUND RD. P.O. BOX 13819 MILWAUKEE, WI 53213

Visit Hal Leonard online at www.halleonard.com

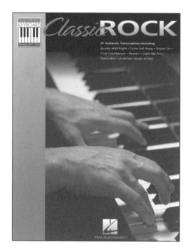

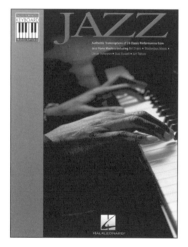